Terrorism

ADAM HIBBERT

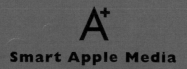

Smart Apple Media

Library of Congress Cataloging-in-Publication Data

Hibbert, Adam, 1968-
Terrorism / Adam Hibbert.
v. cm. — (In the news)
Includes bibliographical references and index.
Contents: What is terrorism?—How do terrorists work?—Who would be a terrorist?—Fighting for the people—Holy
terror—Eco-terrorism—Random individuals—Paying for terror—Limits to terror—Casefile: Northern Ireland—
Countering terrorism—Achieving peace—Terror tomorrow.
ISBN 1-58340-395-7
1. Terrorism—Juvenile literature. 2. Terrorists—Juvenile literature. 3. Political violence—Juvenile literature. 4. Terrorism—
Prevention—Juvenile literature. [1. Terrorism.]

HV6431.H53 2003
303.6'25—dc21   2002042792

2 4 6 8 9 7 5 3 1

Acknowledgments:
Amar Amar/Sipa/Rex Features: front cover, 13b. Paul Baldesare/Photofusion: 9t (posed by models).
Rogan Coles/Sipa/Rex Features: 26t. EPA/PA Photos: 10t. Paul Faith/PA Photos: 23t.
Richard Gardener/Rex Features: 22b. Francesco Guidicini/Rex Features: 10b.
Menahem Kahana/Reuters/Popperfoto: 4bl. Alan Lewis/Rex Features: 27b.
Patsy Lynch/Rex Features: 12b. Paul McErlane/Reuters/Popperfoto: 22t.
D. Miller/Greenpeace: 15t. Aladin Abdel Naby/Reuters/Popperfoto: 21t.
Yellupiltei Prabhakhran/Rex: 4tr. Rafiqur Rahman/Reuters/Popperfoto: 28t.
Andrew Shaw/Rex Features: 28b. Rex Features: 14b, 16t, 17t, 18t, 19b.
Sipa/Rex Features: 6t, 7b, 8r, 9b, 25b, 29b. Ray Stubblebine/Reuters/Popperfoto: 5b.
Sutcliffe/Sipa/Rex Features: 16b. The Times/Rex Features: 20b.
F. Zabaci/Rex Features: 24t.

CONTENTS

WHAT IS TERRORISM?

PUT SIMPLY, *terrorism means using violence to get what one wants. Terrorist groups have political or religious beliefs that they try to force onto society by threatening or using violence. Unlike guerrilla armies, terrorist groups normally do not expect to win by military success alone. They aim to scare the public into changing the way society works.*

POLITICS AND TERROR

Not so many centuries ago, it was normal to use violence to control society. The question of who ruled was decided by battling armies, and rulers could kill or throw out anyone who was against them. Most modern societies do not allow violence to be used to decide how a country should be run. Political decisions in democracies are made by talking through people's different opinions, finding compromises, and voting.

⬆ *The Tamil Tigers fight to gain power for the minority Tamils in Sri Lanka. As well as guerrilla warfare, they use bombs and other terrorist tactics.*

⬇ *Yasser Arafat (left) receives the Nobel Peace Prize in 1994. He is the leader of the Palestine Liberation Organization (PLO), originally a terrorist group, which abandoned violence in hope of a peaceful settlement of the Israel-Palestine dispute.*

MODERN TERRORISM

Even in democracies, some people think that the system is unfair and decide to use violence to achieve their goals. Anarchists, who believe we would be better off without any sort of government, were among the first modern groups to use terrorism. Extreme anarchists killed leading government figures, such as Russia's Tsar Alexander I in 1881.

INVENTING TERROR

Most modern terrorist methods were invented in the early part of the 20th century. Irish opponents to British rule in Ireland invented a time-bomb, and the French Resistance perfected secret warfare under the Nazi occupation of World War II. Terrorists search for new methods to gain their ends. Using hijacked passenger jets and their fuel as flying bombs is a new idea, used against the United States by Islamic extremists with catastrophic results in September 2001.

⬇ The World Trade Center in New York was destroyed in 2001 by a terrorist suicide attack.

NEW WORLD ORDER

The Cold War between the Soviet Union (USSR) and the West had a big impact on terrorism. Each side offered weapons and money to any terrorist groups causing damage to the "enemy." When the USSR collapsed in 1991 and became Russia once more, the reasons for supporting terror also ended. Some terror groups gave up, and others turned to negotiations and normal politics. But new groups began to form. . . .

GET THE FACTS STRAIGHT

Terrorism is hard to make statistics about, because different experts have different ideas about what counts as terrorism. Some facts are clearer than others.

● Around the world, roughly 50% of terrorist actions are bombings, 20% are shootings, and 30% are kidnappings, hostage-takings, or hijackings.

● About 20% of terrorist actions result in someone being killed.

● Of that deadly 20%, the number of people killed has risen dramatically over the last 30 years. Terrorists appear to be less concerned about death tolls than they were during the Cold War.

HOW DO TERRORISTS WORK?

TERRORIST GROUPS *are made up of people who are convinced that society is deeply unfair. They believe normal politics cannot solve the problem, and that this makes it acceptable to break the law to achieve change. This is sometimes called choosing the bullet rather than the ballot box. This choice makes terrorists unpopular, but allows them to make headlines and forces people to listen to their demands.*

⬆ *These Lebanese hijackers held 30 U.S. hostages on a plane in Beirut for 16 days in 1985, demanding the release of prisoners from Israel. In doing so, they also captured the attention of the world's press – note the microphones.*

ORGANIZED TERROR

Like any criminals, terrorists are careful to keep their activities secret from the police. Many terrorist groups are organized like the French Resistance, in units or "cells" of a few terrorists each. Each cell works alone. If undercover policemen or government spies succeed in joining the group, they will find out about only a handful of people, and the other cells can carry on fighting.

MAKING AN IMPACT

About half of all terrorist attacks in the 20th century were bombings. Bombs are well-suited to terrorist activities. They can be set to explode after the terrorists have escaped, or sent through the mail. Normal criminals rarely use bombs. This means that the media are more likely to report a bomb attack, giving the terrorists publicity – one of their main goals.

DIRECT TERROR

Terrorist groups also use guns, which are really useful only for killing people or taking hostages. Using a gun means that a terrorist has to be present at the moment of attack, risking capture or being shot by the police, so guns are normally used only for self-defense, punishing people who betray the group, or robberies to raise funds.

A car bomb planted by Basque nationalist group ETA in Viroia, Spain, in February 2000 killed Member of Parliament Fernando Buesa and his bodyguard. There was a massive demonstration for peace the next day.

WHAT DO YOU THINK?

Would any of the following situations make it acceptable for you to kill people?

- It is made illegal for people of your ethnic identity to have a vote.
- It is made illegal for people of another ethnic identity to have a vote.
- Your community is discriminated against.
- Your religion demands that you fight against an "evil" social practice (such as abortion).
- Your country is occupied by a foreign army.
- Your country is run by foreign businesses.

If you think some of the above are reasons for violence, and others are not, try to describe where the difference lies.

DEATH OR DESTRUCTION?

Some terror groups try to avoid harming or killing people. When they leave a bomb, they call the police and warn them to clear the area before it goes off. This way they can cause damage and create fear without killing innocent people. Other groups believe that they can terrify everyone only by killing as many as possible. But this approach disgusts the public and often even the group's own supporters.

7

TERRORISM OCCURS in various very different places around the world. Terrorist groups are fighting for all sorts of reasons (see pages 10-17) and may even fight each other. But looking at terrorists as a whole, it is possible to see some similarities across all the differences. Terrorism experts can tell us what sorts of people are most likely to become involved in terrorism.

Terrorists may find it easier to attract younger people to their cause, such as these recruits to the Tamil Tigers in Sri Lanka.

RESPECTABLE PEOPLE

Terrorists are often quite wealthy, well-educated people. Many terrorists in the West and the Middle East have been to college. They may learn about their cause as students, or decide to study in order to help their communities. They turn to terrorism because they can't see any other way to make the world a better place.

SIMPLE SOLUTIONS

Most social problems are complicated, but some ways of understanding them provide very simple answers. Young people tend to be more attracted to these simple, black and white ideas. Terrorists usually join their group when they are young and are more likely than older people to volunteer to risk their lives engaging in terror activities.

ALTERNATIVE MORALS

Mainstream society condemns terrorism, but terrorists do not see it that way. Terrorists believe they are heroes fighting for a marginal group. They may think that over time, people will come to see that they were doing the right thing. Terrorist groups motivated by religion can tell themselves that what they are doing is right because it is what God or His prophet demands of them.

GROUP BEHAVIOR

Some scientists study how people behave in groups or gangs. They have found that gang members may use violence against outsiders to prove that they belong to the group. The gang makes its own rules about what's right and wrong, ignoring what outsiders think. Gang members may be violent to outsiders to gain status with their friends in the group. Many of these patterns of behavior can be found within terrorist groups.

⬆ Bullies on the school playground often belong to gangs and egg each other on.

⬇ Rich U.S. teenager Patty Hearst is shown on a Federal Bureau of Investigation (FBI) "Wanted" poster. Her decision to join her kidnappers' terror group shocked the public.

FACING THE ISSUES

There was a trend towards political activism and terrorism among young people in the late 1960s. In America, Patty Hearst, the daughter of a very wealthy family, was held for ransom by an unknown terrorist group calling itself the Symbionese Liberation Army. When terms could not be settled for a payoff, Patty Hearst shocked the public by joining the gang and taking part in a bank robbery. She later explained that she had no choice and served less than three years in prison before being released by President Jimmy Carter in 1979.

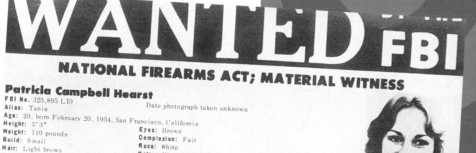

WANTED FBI

NATIONAL FIREARMS ACT; MATERIAL WITNESS

Patricia Campbell Hearst

FBI No. 325,805 L10
Alias: Tania
Age: 20, born February 20, 1954, San Francisco, California
Height: 5'3"
Weight: 110 pounds
Build: Small
Hair: Light brown
Date photograph taken unknown

Eyes: Brown
Complexion: Fair
Race: White
Nationality: American

Scars and Marks: Mole on lower right corner of mouth, scar near right ankle
Remarks: Hair naturally light brown, straight and worn about three inches below shoulders in length, however, may wear wigs, including Afro style, dark brown of medium length; was last seen wearing black sweater, plaid slacks, brown hiking boots and carrying a knife in her belt

CAUTION

THE ABOVE INDIVIDUALS ARE SELF-PROCLAIMED MEMBERS OF THE SYMBIONESE LIBERATION ARMY AND REPORTEDLY HAVE BEEN IN POSSESSION OF NUMEROUS FIREARMS INCLUDING AUTOMATIC WEAPONS. WILLIAM HARRIS AND PATRICIA HEARST ALLEGEDLY HAVE RECENTLY USED GUNS TO AVOID ARREST. ALL THREE SHOULD BE CONSIDERED ARMED AND VERY DANGEROUS.
Federal warrants were issued on May 20, 1974, at Los Angeles, California, charging the Harris' and Hearst with violation of the National Firearms Act. Hearst was also charged in a Federal complaint on April 17, 1974...

SOME TERRORISM AIMS to create an independent country, or nation, for the community it believes it is fighting for. This sort of terrorist group may think of itself as an army of freedom fighters, battling against an occupying force. Their goal is to drive out the existing political system and replace it with one that belongs entirely to their own community.

◣ Kurdish demonstrators show their support for the PKK. One holds a map of the Kurdish nation they want to create. The PKK has an active political wing.

⬆ Mourners still grieve for victims of the Stern Gang, which terrorized Palestinians in 1948 to make way for the nation of Israel.

OUR NATION

Nationalist groups often grow out of a community with its own language and ethnic identity. The PKK, for example, wants to reunite Kurdish people, whose traditional homelands cover parts of Turkey, Iraq, and, to a lesser extent, Syria, Armenia, and Iran.

NATIONALIST STRATEGY

Nationalist terror groups try to make it difficult for existing governments to govern the land they want to "liberate" by causing fear and chaos through terror attacks. They target the existing government's soldiers, policemen, political leaders, and embassies abroad. Perhaps more importantly, they also aim to inspire more of their own community to join their struggle. Many have a political wing that avoids criminal activity and concentrates on spreading their message.

STOP ARM SALES TO TURKEY

GET THE FACTS STRAIGHT

This map shows the main terrorist hot spots around the world. The key below lists the names of the groups and the number of their members, where known.

1 UK/Northern Ireland: Real IRA, Irish Republican Army (70); Continuity IRA (50); LVF, Loyalist Volunteer Force (200); Red Hand Defenders (20?)

2 Israel/Palestine: Hamas (?); PFLP, the Popular Front for the Liberation of Palestine (800); Hizballah (thousands?)

3 Lebanon: Japanese Red Army (8)

4 Afghanistan: Al Qaida (?)

5 Algeria: GIA (Armed Islamic Group) (900–6,000?)

6 Egypt: Islamic Group (5,000)

7 Greece: Revolutionary People's Struggle/17 November (30)

8 Spain: ETA, Basque separatists (600)

9 Sri Lanka: Tamil Tigers (4,000)

10 Turkey: PKK (7,000); Dev Sol (tens?)

11 Mexico: The Zapatista Army (15,000)

12 Colombia: FARC (10,000); ELA (3,000)

13 Peru: Shining Path (3,000); Tupac Amaru (100?)

14 U.S.: Militias, 150 separate organizations (about 30,000, not all terrorists); Earth Liberation Front, ELF (?); Animal Liberation Front, ALF (?)

15 Canada: Justice Department (?)

16 Japan/Australia: Aum Shinrikyo (2,000)

17 South Africa: People Against Gangsterism and Drugs (300)

18 Philippines: New People's Army (10,000); Alex Boncayao Brigade (500); Abyu Sayyaf (200)

RELIGIONS CAN PROVIDE reasons for terrorism, just as political ideas can. One's sense of what is right and what is wrong (morality) often comes from religious ideas. Religion can provide strong moral answers, which are rarely dangerous. Most people of faith tolerate other groups' morals. But when they can't tolerate differences, the result can be violent.

SAVING SOULS

Some Christians believe that the human soul exists once an egg is fertilized in the womb. For them, aborting a fetus is simply murder. In the United States, birth control clinics are sometimes attacked by extremist Christians. Seven medical staff members have been killed since 1993. A few Christians see it as their duty to God to ignore the law and use terrorism to bring an end to abortion.

This protester believes that abortion is a sin. Extreme anti-abortionists have killed medical staff members and thrown acid in the faces of women seeking abortion.

JIHAD

In the Muslim faith, the struggle to do God's work is called *Jihad*. Most Muslims think the struggle is about what they do in their everyday lives – fighting their own weaknesses and treating other people well. But a few believe it also requires "holy war" on those who threaten the Islamic way of life. This belief motivated the attack on the World Trade Center in 2001.

REWARDS IN HEAVEN

New Age cults, such as Japan's Aum Shinrikyo (see page 21), resort to violence because they believe the world is about to end and there is no time to persuade people to join the "true" faith. Other religious terrorists are prepared to go on suicide missions in pursuit of their cause. They normally believe in life after death, so this sacrifice may promise rewards in heaven. Suicide attackers are very hard to stop.

WHAT DO YOU THINK?

- Does every religion provide terrorists with reasons to kill?
- If your religion demanded that you kill, would you question your faith?
- What can religious leaders do to help prevent terrorism?
- Should people be allowed to choose their religion freely, whatever it holds to be true?

Hamas terrorists in the Middle East are inspired to take up violence by their interpretation of Islam. Some will undertake suicide missions.

NATIONALISM AND RELIGION *are not the only things to inspire terrorists – some fight for the Earth itself. Extreme forms of environmentalism can make people think it is acceptable to kill or injure others to protect the planet from human activity.*

EXTREME GREEN

Environmental terrorism is a new trend and is still very rare. Most green activists believe that normal politics and peaceful protests have begun to deliver some of their ambitions. But a group in the United States known as the Earth Liberation Front (ELF) carries out arson attacks on buildings. So far, the ELF appears not to have caused any serious injuries or deaths.

ANIMAL RIGHTS FIGHTS

The Animal Liberation Front (ALF) started in Britain and spread to Canada and the United States. Most of its activities involve no violence to people – for example, breaking into laboratories to liberate animals. But ALF activists have also beaten up businessmen. The murder of U.S. academic Dr. Hyram Kitchen in 1990 has been linked to animal rights terrorists.

TERROR OR PROTEST?

Animal rights activists may protest at the homes of scientists involved in animal research. It is certainly scary for scientists' families, but is this terrorism? Another tactic is the hunger strike. British firebomber Barry Thorne starved himself to death in prison in 2001 in protest against government policy on animal research.

⬇ *This car was bombed by the ALF in Bristol in 1990. It belonged to a veterinarian. A baby was injured by the blast.*

↑ *Greenpeace's* Rainbow Warrior *lies half-submerged in the water after being bombed by French secret agents.*

WHO'S THE TERRORIST?

In 1985, the environmental action group Greenpeace sent a ship, the *Rainbow Warrior*, to protest French nuclear tests in the Pacific Ocean. When it docked in New Zealand, a team of French secret agents fixed explosives to the hull and sank the boat at midnight, when the crew was settling down to sleep. French prime minister Laurent Fabius stated in September 1985 that his country had been guilty of "state terrorism."

FACING THE ISSUES

In Britain, Colin Blakemore is one of a few research scientists who have tried to oppose the claims of animal rights activists. But by becoming well known as a person who supports the use of animals in medical research, he has become a target for animal rights terrorists. Vandalism at his home, death threats, and kidnap threats against his children have forced him to have 24-hour police protection. Blakemore's experience scares other researchers into keeping quiet about their work.

TERRORISM IS CHEAP and easy compared to politics, especially for those whose political ideas are not popular with the general public. In some cases, the political ideas that drive a person to terrorism are so marginal that they decide to act alone, with no group to slow them down. They make their own weapons and choose their own targets.

← Timothy McVeigh was executed in June 2001 for setting a car bomb in Oklahoma in 1995. The bomb killed 168 people, including 19 children.

↑ Militia men in the U.S. believe they are defending the country's democracy from a powerful central government. Most are law-abiding.

MILITIA MAN

The United States experienced very little terrorism within its borders until April 1995. Then a huge car bomb exploded outside a government building in Oklahoma. The bomb was set by a young man named Timothy McVeigh. He believed he was fighting to free the U.S. from a shadowy conspiracy that controlled the government, an idea popular among the U.S.'s many amateur militias.

RACE WAR

Three nail-bombs exploded in London in 1999. Each had a different minority as its target – Afro-Caribbeans, Asians, and gays – but killed and injured all kinds of Britons. They were set by David Copeland, a young man with a history of involvement in British fascist groups. Acting alone, he hoped to provoke a race war to make these fascist groups more popular.

➦ This pub in central London was targeted in 1999 by a lone nail-bomber, influenced by fascist political groups.

LONE BOMBER

In America, an ex-university professor known as the Unabomber had a 20-year career making bombs, attacking people he thought were destroying the planet. He killed 3 and injured 23, but because he acted alone, there were no clues. He was caught in 1996 only after his brother recognized his handwriting on a letter that was printed in the newspapers.

RESPONDING TO RANDOMNESS

Governments can target known terrorist groups. They only have to monitor a few telephones, look for informants in particular places, or plant spies in a known community to begin to gather evidence. But random terrorists are almost impossible to detect. A government would need to have extreme powers to keep an eye on each and every one of its citizens. As Jay Robert Nash put it in his book *Terrorism in the 20th Century*: "It is the lone terrorist that all fear most."

GET THE FACTS STRAIGHT

- Bombings in the U.S. rose from fewer than 1,000 in 1990 to nearly 5,000 separate incidents in 1998.
- A lone bomber, Eric Rudolph, is still being hunted by the FBI for bomb attacks on abortion clinics and the Atlanta Olympic Games in 1996.
- Terrorists acting alone are thought to use bomb-making information from the Internet. There are several Web sites that give this type of information. But amateur bombs are very unpredictable and often explode while being built.

17

Smuggling illegal drugs, such as this valuable shipment intercepted by customs officers, is a way for terrorists to raise cash.

TERRORISTS NEED MONEY to buy guns and explosives and to keep their operations secret. Sometimes entire active units of up to 10 terrorists will be sent to another country to attack a target, with all the expenses of air travel and fake passports. "Safe houses" cost money, too – here, sympathizers are paid to look after terrorists on the run.

GET THE FACTS STRAIGHT

In 1990, the British government estimated the IRA had $3.3 million turnover per year, including earnings from these sources:
- $650,000 from tax fraud
- $650,000 from legitimate companies
- $650,000 from illegal bars and casinos
- $375,000 from smuggling and video piracy
- $300,000 from extortion and protection rackets
- $60,000 from donations

CHEAP AND TERRIBLE

It is possible to build bombs cheaply, so even groups with very little money can cause some damage and gain some publicity. But most groups find ways to raise cash from people who are sympathetic to their ideas. Terrorists may set up fake charities to obtain donations, pretending that the money is going to good causes such as orphans or refugees.

DEEP POCKETS

One terrorist group, Al Qaida, has been financed by the personal wealth of its leader, Osama Bin Laden. His family's successful Saudi Arabian business is thought to have earned Bin Laden more than $200 million. But even Al Qaida encourages the groups it sponsors to raise their own cash. Very wealthy individuals usually use their money for political influence, not terrorism.

BLACK MARKET

The need for secrecy may put terrorists in contact with organized crime. For example, terrorist groups may need help with money laundering or illegal arms purchases, and often become expert smugglers. Making money through drug smuggling or even armed robberies is common among Western terror groups. In South America, kidnapping rich tourists for ransom has also funded terrorism.

SECRET WARFARE

Since the end of the Cold War, it is less common to find that terrorists are funded by foreign governments, but it still happens. Countries that would be condemned for attacking an enemy openly can pursue a secret war by giving money or guns to a terrorist group in the country they want to attack. It's a risky strategy – countries caught doing this have been banned from international trade and even bombed.

↙ *A 5.5 ton (5 t) shipment of guns and missiles from Colonel Muammar Gaddafi, dictator of Libya, was intercepted on its way to the IRA in 1973.*

GET THE FACTS STRAIGHT

- The President of the German Central Bank, Ernst Welteke, said that movements in share prices for airlines, insurance, and oil suggest that some investors knew in advance about the attacks against the U.S. on September 11. Did terror networks make money betting on the stock markets in September 2001?

- Studying cashflows to identify terrorist funding may be of little use. Some terror networks employ the "chop" system of payment, where money never changes hands. Instead, a password is given to access gold or diamonds that remain in the care of a third party.

- The European Union froze bank accounts containing about $40 million in September 2001. The money was linked to Taliban leaders in Afghanistan.

19

LIMITS TO TERROR

IN THE 1990S, after the collapse of the Soviet Union, many people were afraid that Russian nuclear weapons would fall into the wrong hands. It is easy to imagine terrorists secretly having very destructive weapons. Scare stories help to sell newspapers, but the truth is usually far less worrying.

➡️ *Terrorists don't need WMDs to make an impact. This gun attack at Luxor in 1997 killed 58 tourists, threatening Egypt's vital $4 billion tourist industry.*

⬇️ *Nuclear technology such as this power plant is far beyond the finances or know-how of any known terrorist group.*

SELF-DESTRUCTION

Almost all terrorists take pride in their achievements, believing them to be part of a just war. This acts as a limit on the amount of violence in which they can indulge. Using nuclear weapons, for example, would offend the rest of the world so deeply that the terrorists would risk losing their supporters, exposing them to capture and making their goals impossible to achieve.

ROUGH AND READY

In reality, terror groups prefer to use conventional weapons. They carry fewer risks than weapons of mass destruction (WMDs), which only skilled technicians can operate. So far, even the most sophisticated terror attacks have used conventional technology. High-tech weapons require scientific research that few countries, let alone outlaw groups, can afford.

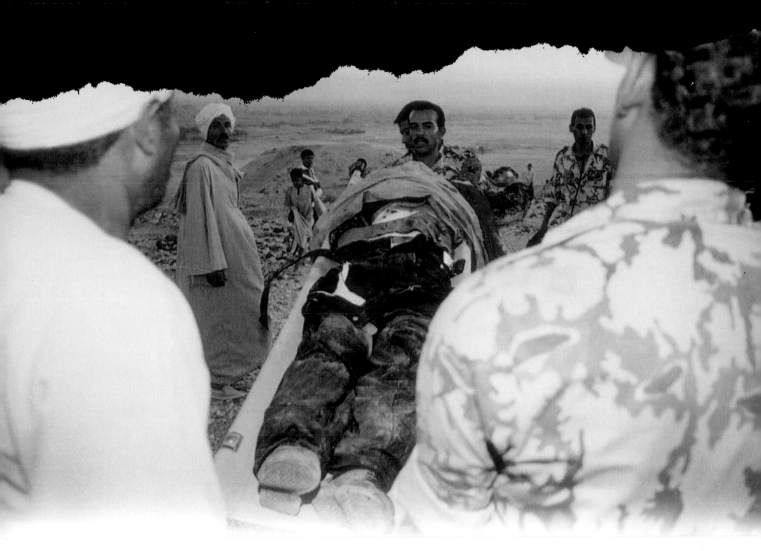

CHEMICAL AND BIOLOGICAL WEAPONS

Following the attacks on the U.S. in September 2001, many businesses were closed because of fears of further terror attacks using anthrax, a natural bacterium that can be deadly for humans. A few people were infected by low-tech anthrax letter attacks. But it turned out that only the U.S. and Russia had the technology necessary to turn anthrax into a WMD.

LOW TECH

Guns are easy to use but can be hard to come by. However, information on how to make bombs is readily available in any industrial society. Bombmakers Dominic McGlinchy and Francis Hughes are said to have created one type of booby-trap bomb after reading the Ladybird children's book, *Batteries, Bulbs and Magnets*. The trigger they invented was made from a clothespin. Today the Internet has several bomb-making Web sites.

FACING THE ISSUES

Aum Shinrikyo, an apocalyptic cult based in Japan, is the only terror group to date to have used a serious chemical weapon. In 1993, the cult used some of its $1 billion wealth to buy Banjawarn Sheep Station in Western Australia. It used the farm to test nerve gases on animals. Then, in March 1995, the cult attempted to gas thousands of commuters in Tokyo's underground railway. By luck, just 12 people died, though 5,500 needed hospital treatment. The cult immediately lost its influence, its supporters dropped away, and its leader was arrested. This kind of result is a powerful deterrent against terror groups using WMDs.

TERRORISM HAS existed in Irish politics for almost the entire history of Britain's involvement in Ireland. Recent violence began in 1969, when Northern Ireland's Catholics were demonstrating for equal rights with Protestants. The Catholic civil rights movement met with violent attacks from loyalist extremists, prompting the British to send troops in to restore order.

⬇ ⬈ *Symbols of division: the opposing communities in Belfast create these murals to mark their turf and announce their political beliefs.*

WHAT'S THE ISSUE?

There are different ways to understand why people turned to terrorism in Northern Ireland. It can appear that the reason is religious prejudice between Catholic and Protestant Christians. But most people, including the terrorists themselves, see it as a conflict between those who want to remain loyal to Britain – loyalists – and those who want to join the Republic of Ireland – republicans.

HOW DID IT HAPPEN?

Most Catholics welcomed British troops in 1969, thinking they would offer protection from loyalists. But the troops soon came into conflict with republicans as well, killing several unarmed Catholic demonstrators on January 30, 1972 – remembered as "Bloody Sunday." The violence spiraled out of control, reaching a peak with the IRA's attempted assassination of the entire British Cabinet in Brighton in October 1984.

⬆ Loyalist protests in 2001 against Catholic children walking to school through their housing estate highlighted Northern Ireland's deep divisions.

SOME KEY EVENTS

August 1968: First civil rights march in Belfast

April 1969: 500 British troops arrive, sent in response to unrest

December 1969: The IRA takes up arms

August 1971: 300 terror suspects held without trial. Riots follow

January 1972: "Bloody Sunday"

December 1976: Act outlaws discrimination in employment on religious grounds

May 1981: Republican prisoner Bobby Sands is first of 10 to die on hunger strike

November 1985: Anglo-Irish Agreement creates joint council for cross-border matters

March 1993: Warrington bomb kills two children, prompting more calls for a ceasefire

December 1993: The Downing Street Declaration states that Britain has no "selfish, strategic or economic interests" in Northern Ireland

August 1994: IRA announces ceasefire

October 1994: Loyalists announce ceasefire

January 1995: British troops stop daytime patrols in Belfast

November 1997: IRA splits; Real IRA forms

April 1998: Good Friday Agreement amends constitutions of Britain and Ireland towards reconciliation

August 1998: Real IRA kills 29 and injures 200 in Omagh

December 1999: Northern Ireland Assembly is granted control of Northern Ireland

WHO ARE THE GROUPS?

The Irish Republican Army (IRA) was the largest terrorist organization in Northern Ireland. It began by attacking loyalists and agents of the British government, but turned to killing random British citizens on the mainland. The IRA aimed to scare the British public into accepting its demands. Loyalist groups, such as the Loyalist Volunteer Force (LVF), killed leading republicans and random Catholics.

PROCESSED PEACE

After more than 20 years of sickening violence, the main groups involved in terror declared ceasefires at the end of 1994. This peace process has not been easy. Some people could not be persuaded to join talks – a splinter group of IRA militants, called the Real IRA, still bombs Britain. And both sides have since committed more atrocities, though the negotiations have continued. In October 2001, the IRA put some of its weapons "beyond use."

COUNTERING TERRORISM

British soldiers stormed the Iranian embassy in London in 1980. Many governments have special forces such as these soldiers, who are trained to combat terrorists. Their identities are kept secret to prevent revenge attacks.

TERRORISM IS A DIFFICULT problem for governments to deal with. Unlike other criminals, terrorists are normally very well armed, and may enjoy some support in the communities they believe they are fighting for. This means that, as well as a military response, governments sometimes have to negotiate with terrorist leaders as if they were legitimate politicians.

FIRE WITH FIRE

Counter-terrorism normally has a military aspect. In South America, the Colombian government has created successful anti-terror hit squads, which specialize in finding and, if necessary, killing terrorists. The trouble is that if governments engage in open warfare with terrorists, they risk confirming the terrorists' idea that they are soldiers.

INTELLIGENCE

A more reliable way to combat terrorist groups is to gather information about their activities and leaders. Governments that make high-profile arrests among terrorist groups, as Spain has done with the Basque separatist group ETA, stand a better chance of controlling the problem. Imprisoning terrorists as murderers is much more effective than killing them and making them heroes.

DEFENSE

Governments can also increase security on terrorist targets. Increasing security can be costly, though – not just in money but, more importantly, in the loss of freedom for ordinary citizens. Terrorism experts have shown that increased security on one type of target encourages terrorists to look for easier ones. This can result in the public feeling more terrorized than before.

THE LAST RESORT

Recent terrorism has tended to come from groups that have no clear goals or identity. It can be hard to know how to discourage this type of terrorism. One way may be to promise a terrible response – to punish the community that the terrorist claims to be fighting for. But this terrorist solution may create more hatred and may inspire more people to become terrorists themselves.

FACING THE ISSUES

Al Qaida is the name of a loose network of terrorists thought to be responsible for 2001's suicide attacks on the Pentagon and World Trade Center. Though they share training facilities and perhaps some financing from leader Osama Bin Laden, the different units of the network are not dependent on each other. This makes it very hard to defeat the entire network. The biggest steps forward have been made by bringing more and more countries into an information-sharing coalition. The improved intelligence allows all governments to act whenever one part of Al Qaida plots an attack.

The Basque terror group FTA has suffered from careful targeting by Spanish and French special forces. But killing terrorists can make them into martyrs.

ACHIEVING PEACE

The 1994 election in South Africa.

THE MOST SUCCESSFUL strategy for bringing an end to terrorism is to persuade terrorists to give up arms in favor of normal political argument. Governments have to be brave to do this, since there is usually widespread public disgust at the idea of negotiating with the "murderers."

STARTING TO TALK

At first, it is necessary to build trust among terrorists that talks will be taken seriously, and that real gains can be won from the negotiations. Governments cannot make big concessions to terrorists without looking weak. It is hard for terrorist leaders, too. If they agree to talk without convincing all of their members, a group often splits off to continue fighting.

FACING THE ISSUES

The African National Congress (ANC) was set up in 1912 to campaign for equal rights in South Africa for the black majority. The white government banned the ANC in 1960. A vicious war began between black activists and the state. The ANC set up an illegal military wing, Umkonto We Sizwe, or Spear of the Nation, under Nelson Mandela. The government created secret death squads, such as Colonel Eugene de Kock's Vlakplaas group, to kill black political leaders. The two sides eventually met in peace talks, resulting in the granting of voting rights to non-whites, and Mandela was elected South Africa's first black president in 1994.

- In what ways do you think terrorists who remain active during a peace process can affect the outcome? Do they have any power?
- How do you think South Africa's Truth and Reconciliation hearings help the country move on?
- Would you negotiate if someone who shot a relative of yours was involved in the discussion with you? If so, in what circumstances?
- "Once a terrorist, always a terrorist." What is your reaction to this statement?

ROOM FOR AGREEMENT?

The key to achieving peace is finding a compromise that all the parties can live with. In northern Spain, the government in 1978 handed many of its functions over to the Basque people to decide for themselves in a sort of regional government. This was enough for most Basque people to stop supporting terror. But there seems to be less room for compromise between, for example, Israel and Palestine.

BUILDING BRIDGES

As long as peace holds and people are hopeful that politics can provide an answer, it is possible to start healing the wounds that terror campaigns caused. In South Africa, the new government held Truth and Reconciliation hearings, which required people from both sides to confess to their terror activities so that the country could put old injustices behind it and move on.

When terrorists' own communities demand peace, terrorist groups may call ceasefires and begin peace talks.

NEW CONSENSUS SAYS: STOP THE KILLING TO START THE PEACE

TERROR TOMORROW

THE END OF THE COLD WAR has brought big changes in world terrorism. It is extremely difficult to look ahead at the start of this new era to see where these changes will lead. If this book had been written before September 11, 2001, for example, it could not have foreseen that America would experience such a devastating attack.

⬇ The IRA detonated a car bomb in London in 1993 to make a deep crater, bursting the main water supply and severing telecommunications cables.

⬆ Pakistani supporters of Osama Bin Laden downloaded his picture with Bert from Sesame Street from a humorous Web site. They used it to make protest placards, unaware of the joke intended. The Internet may play a more serious role in terrorism in the future.

GET THE FACTS STRAIGHT

Bar chart of deaths per year as a result of terrorist activity.

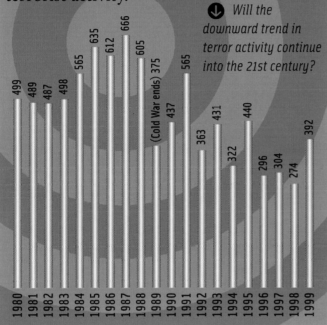

⬇ *Will the downward trend in terror activity continue into the 21st century?*

1980	1981	1982	1983	1984	1985	1986	1987	1988	1989	1990	1991	1992	1993	1994	1995	1996	1997	1998	1999
499	489	487	498	565	635	612	666	605	(Cold War ends) 375	437	565	363	431	322	440	296	304	274	392

TECHNO TERROR

Some governments are preparing for terrorist attacks on computer networks. America's Defense Information Systems Agency has set up a unit called the Red Team, which tests security by secretly hacking government computers. In April 1993, the IRA's Bishopsgate bomb in London was designed to sever telecom cables beneath the road to cause chaos in computer banking systems.

GLOBAL INTELLIGENCE

In response to the changing patterns of terror, the major countries of the world have put more emphasis on sharing information and monitoring flows of people and money around the world. This international cooperation, especially if it involves the Middle East, is vital to thwart terrorist activity.

↘ *U.S. President Bush and Russian President Putin traveled to China in 2001 to improve cooperation with their traditional enemy.*

WORLD CONFLICT

Some activists in poor countries want to resist Western influence. Before 1989, they could use the competition between the two superpowers, the U.S. and USSR, to win themselves some independence. It is now much harder for them to stand up for themselves by legitimate means, and this frustration may lead more of them to resort to terrorism.

PUBLIC DISINTEREST

Activists within Western countries also face new frustrations. Public interest in politics has collapsed across the Western world, making it harder to win support for political ideas by acceptable methods. As politics become more distant from people's daily lives, conspiracy theory groups such as America's militias may become more credible, causing more damage.

GLOSSARY

abortion: Stopping a pregnancy by removing the developing baby (fetus) from the womb.

activists: People who take action to achieve their political goals, peacefully or otherwise.

anarchists: People who believe that there should be no government at all and that the way people live is a matter of individual responsibility alone.

anthrax: A harmful bacterium that can cause skin ulcers and lung failure. Anthrax can be treated with antibiotics.

civil rights: The rights of a citizen, such as the freedom to vote, to debate, to move around, and to be political, without interference by the government.

coalition: A group of countries or organizations working together for a specific goal.

Cold War: Historically, the conflict between the U.S. and its allies and the Soviet Union, which never quite turned into direct attacks. It evolved after World War II and ended in 1989 when the Soviet Union began to collapse.

conspiracy theory: The idea that a few powerful people plot to keep the truth from the public or to control whole societies.

conventional weapons: Weapons using relatively simple technology, from bows and arrows to bombs and missiles, whose destructive powers are limited to fairly small areas.

cult: A small, extreme religion or section of a religion, often following one charismatic leader and with beliefs that isolate it from the rest of society.

democracy: A society in which government decisions are made by the citizens, directly by voting, or indirectly by electing representatives.

embassy: A government office placed in a foreign country to build friendship and trade with that country.

environmentalism: Campaigning to protect nature from changes caused by people.

fascism: A political ideology that believes in a very powerful government and extremely racist policies.

guerrilla army: A hit-and-run army, often unofficial, that uses small-scale attacks to make life difficult for its enemy.

hijack: To take control of an airplane or other vehicle by force, often to hold hostages and make ransom demands.

militia: A group of citizens trained as soldiers. In the U.S., militias are loyal to particular states and may oppose a central U.S. government.

money laundering: Changing illegally-earned money into "clean" money by filtering it through cash businesses and bank accounts.

nationalists: Persons or groups who want to create their own nation or to free an existing nation from foreign rulers.

organized crime: Crimes carried out by criminals organized as a family or a business, often with a powerful crime "boss."

refugee: A person who is forced to leave his or her home nation to start a new life in another country.

society: A country, community, or group of people organized according to certain rules.

splinter group: A relatively small number of members of a group who break away to form their own group.

weapons of mass destruction (WMDs): High-tech methods of causing deaths by the thousands – for example, nuclear, chemical, or biological weapons.

FURTHER INFORMATION

INDEPENDENT ORGANIZATIONS

Conflict Archive on the Internet
An academic resource with detailed information on the conflict in Northern Ireland, including accessible data on casualties.
cain.ulst.ac.uk

Electronic Frontiers Foundation
A U.S.-based civil rights site, with thought-provoking articles on the many ways counter-terrorism can undermine liberty. Enter "terrorism" in the Index Search to find related articles.
www.eff.org

The International Institute of Strategic Studies (IISS)
A London-based think tank specializing in international security issues, which published a paper examining trends in terrorism.
www.iiss.org

Israel/Palestine Center for Research and Information (IPCRI)
A joint Palestinian-Israeli think tank that was created to find solutions to the Arab/Israeli conflict. See especially their peace education project for schools.
www.ipcri.org/index1.html

National Abortion Federation
An organization of abortion practitioners in the U.S. with an up-to-date archive on anti-abortion terror activity.
www.prochoice.org

The Terrorism Research Center
A terrorism consultancy bringing together research and expertise from several countries, including the UK, U.S., France, and Australia. Has some archive material and a very useful links page.
www.terrorism.com

GOVERNMENT SITES

The British Northern Ireland Office
Slow but well-connected government pages on Northern Ireland.
www.nio.gov.uk

Travel Advice
Comprehensive travel advice from the British government about danger zones around the world.
www.fco.gov.uk/travel/countryadvice.asp

The U.S. Counterterrorism Office
The official U.S. government site for terrorism reports. The annual report identifies trends and lists organizations.
www.state.gov/s/ct/

INTERNATIONAL ORGANIZATIONS

The United Nations
These two UN sites have useful information on terrorism and its causes:

The UN Action Against Terrorism
Updates on new measures and reports on what UN commissioners are doing to combat terrorism.
www.un.org/terrorism/

Question of Palestine
A UN Web site reviewing the history and current status of the Arab/Israeli conflict.
www.un.org/Depts/dpa/qpal/

INDEX